The Disciples

The Twelve Disciples, sometimes named the Apostles, were the men chosen by Jesus, the Son of the living God. That alone, if there were no other reasons, warrants a Christian's special and specific consideration.

Their selection was of unusual importance to the Master, for so much would depend on these men who would be His own intimate companions. And Jesus did not choose them in any careless or casual manner.

These disciples were not alike, a fact which should encourage every believing Christian. Any one can be a follower of the Lord Jesus Christ. There is no one class, conformity to rank, title or classification. In "The Holy Band" there is portrayed the wide variety among men, thereby revealing clearly that the call to discipleship is not channeled in any identical manner or by a pattern which is always the same.

Four were fishermen. One was a tax collector. Not one was a priest or ordained clergyman. There were two sets of brothers. Yet, together they responded to the warm friendship of the Christ, and through their lives sounded the strains of new and beautiful spiritual melodies.

Jesus was Teacher, who inspired, who challenged these men. Jesus was Friend, who counseled and consoled them in their hours of victory and in their depths of despair. Jesus was Redeemer, who transformed their loyalties and led them to the Father Above, who in turn gave them peace and pardon.

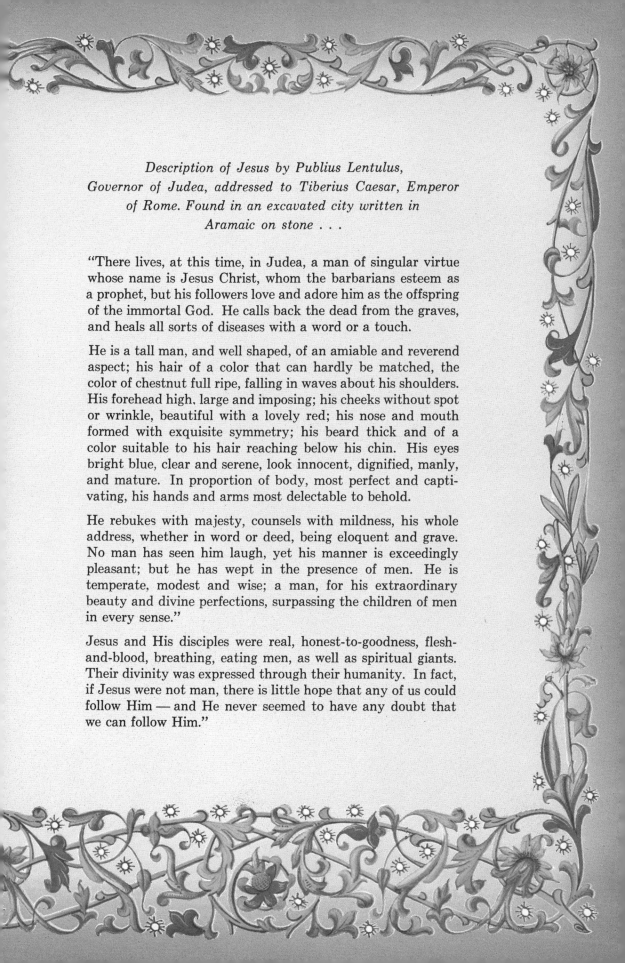

Description of Jesus by Publius Lentulus,
Governor of Judea, addressed to Tiberius Caesar, Emperor
of Rome. Found in an excavated city written in
Aramaic on stone . . .

"There lives, at this time, in Judea, a man of singular virtue whose name is Jesus Christ, whom the barbarians esteem as a prophet, but his followers love and adore him as the offspring of the immortal God. He calls back the dead from the graves, and heals all sorts of diseases with a word or a touch.

He is a tall man, and well shaped, of an amiable and reverend aspect; his hair of a color that can hardly be matched, the color of chestnut full ripe, falling in waves about his shoulders. His forehead high, large and imposing; his cheeks without spot or wrinkle, beautiful with a lovely red; his nose and mouth formed with exquisite symmetry; his beard thick and of a color suitable to his hair reaching below his chin. His eyes bright blue, clear and serene, look innocent, dignified, manly, and mature. In proportion of body, most perfect and captivating, his hands and arms most delectable to behold.

He rebukes with majesty, counsels with mildness, his whole address, whether in word or deed, being eloquent and grave. No man has seen him laugh, yet his manner is exceedingly pleasant; but he has wept in the presence of men. He is temperate, modest and wise; a man, for his extraordinary beauty and divine perfections, surpassing the children of men in every sense."

Jesus and His disciples were real, honest-to-goodness, flesh-and-blood, breathing, eating men, as well as spiritual giants. Their divinity was expressed through their humanity. In fact, if Jesus were not man, there is little hope that any of us could follow Him — and He never seemed to have any doubt that we can follow Him."

Andrew

*John 6:8, 9 — One of the Disciples, Andrew, Simon
Peter's brother, said to Him: "... There is a lad
here who has five barley loaves and two fish,
but what are they among so many."*

Andrew's dominant spiritual attribute is STRENGTH.

The first real friend that Jesus had was Andrew, and the
strength he showed was primarily strength of character. Like
Peter, his brother, for whom he worked, he was a fisherman on
the sea of Galilee.

Andrew was called "the introducer", for it was he who
introduced his brother to Jesus, as soon as he knew that this
was the true "Messiah". He brought before Him, the little boy
with the loaves and fishes, when Jesus fed the 5,000 hungry
people. It was he that introduced the first of the Greeks to
Jesus — and it is believed that when he went to bring his
brother, Peter, to Jesus, John went with him and called his
brother James. Andrew was there when John the Baptist
baptized Jesus in the River Jordan.

Many Scotch and Russian Christians have Andrew as their
patron saint.

Andrew was a gentleman, for he did all things with gentleness
and love. He met his death because he refused to worship a
pagan god. Forgiving to the end, his last words, according to
legend, were: "Would, Father, that I had time to teach truth
to my murderers . . ."

Bartholomew

(or Nathanael)

John 1:47 — Jesus saw Nathanael coming to Him, and
said of him: "Behold an Israelite indeed, in whom
is no guile."

Bartholomew has IMAGINATION as his dominant spiritual attribute.

The quality of IMAGINATION represented in Bartholomew was the divine "imaging" quality of creativeness through which spiritual ideas are made manifest. When Philip found Nathanael sitting under the fig tree, and told him he had found the Messiah, Nathanael's first reply was: "Can anything good come out of Nazareth?"

Nathanael was one of the first six men chosen as a Disciple by Jesus, who recognized him as a man of vision and imagination. Philip bade him "Come and see," and when he had come to Christ, and was convinced, he declared: "... thou art the Son of God; thou art King of Israel."

As Bartholomew, after Pentecost, he traveled with Philip throughout the East — to Mesopotamia, Persia, Egypt, and to Armenia where he was "martyred."

John

I John 4:8 — John the Disciple says, "God is Love".

John's dominant spiritual attribute is LOVE.

Known as "the beloved Disciple", John represents the highest power and the strongest Christian quality, LOVE. He was the son of the fisherman, Zebedee, and he and his brother James, once called "sons of thunder", were strong, brave men who sailed the sea in little fishing boats in stormy as well as good weather.

John showed his courage and devotion in many ways. It was he who stayed at the foot of the cross, comforting Mary, Mother of Jesus. John was the first to recognize Jesus after His resurrection. Returning from a fishing trip, he looked toward the shore and saw the lone figure of a man whom he recognized as Jesus. In this portrait, we see John looking toward the shore and saying: "It is our Lord."

Jesus loved this Disciple as a brother, and it was into John's care that he committed his mother, saying: "Woman, behold thy son!"

John lived to be a very old man. The Bible tells us he was seen in Jerusalem fifteen years after Paul's first visit. He was sent into exile on the Island of Patmos, and it was there that he wrote the inspired Book of the Bible, "The Revelations."

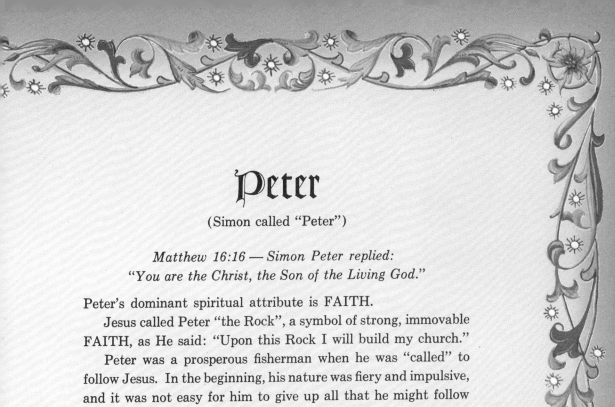

Peter

(Simon called "Peter")

Matthew 16:16 — Simon Peter replied:
"You are the Christ, the Son of the Living God."

Peter's dominant spiritual attribute is FAITH.

Jesus called Peter "the Rock", a symbol of strong, immovable FAITH, as He said: "Upon this Rock I will build my church."

Peter was a prosperous fisherman when he was "called" to follow Jesus. In the beginning, his nature was fiery and impulsive, and it was not easy for him to give up all that he might follow the Master. Yet he renounced the world, became a brave and worthy Disciple, and finally was chosen by Jesus to lead the Disciples in the work they must do after the crucifixion.

Peter was told by Jesus that he would "deny Him three times", which he did. He suffered great remorse, even though it may be, as some scholars believe, that he had been "ordered" by Jesus to do this. In any case, Peter became a great, inspired leader — not only for the original little band of Disciples who became "Apostles" — but for "The Seventy" other Disciples sent forth, and for all the early Christians who followed *Jesus the Christ* even in the face of persecution, exile and death.

Peter preached the gospel all of his life, going forth as the others did, to carry the Word of God as a Light to people in darkness, even giving his life in the end, as Jesus did. Mark served as Peter's interpreter and writer. The Gospel of Mark, based upon Peter's Aramaic records, is known as "the Gospel of action."

Jude

(or Thaddaeus)

John 14:22—Judas (not Iscariot) said unto Him, "Lord, how is it that you will manifest yourself to us, and not to the world?"

Jude's dominant spiritual attribute is RENUNCIATION.

Jude, also called "Judas" should not be confused with Judas Iscariot who betrayed Jesus. Very little is heard of him, except indirectly, but he was a brother of James the Less, and is believed to have been of the family of Jesus.

In the Epistle of JUDE, he warns against false values and penalties for believing in the false gods of a material world, as revealed by history. He urged the ungodly to renounce all which would separate them from the goodness of God.

After Pentecost, Jude traveled to Arabia, Syria, and to Persia, where he is believed to have preached the gospel until the end of his life.

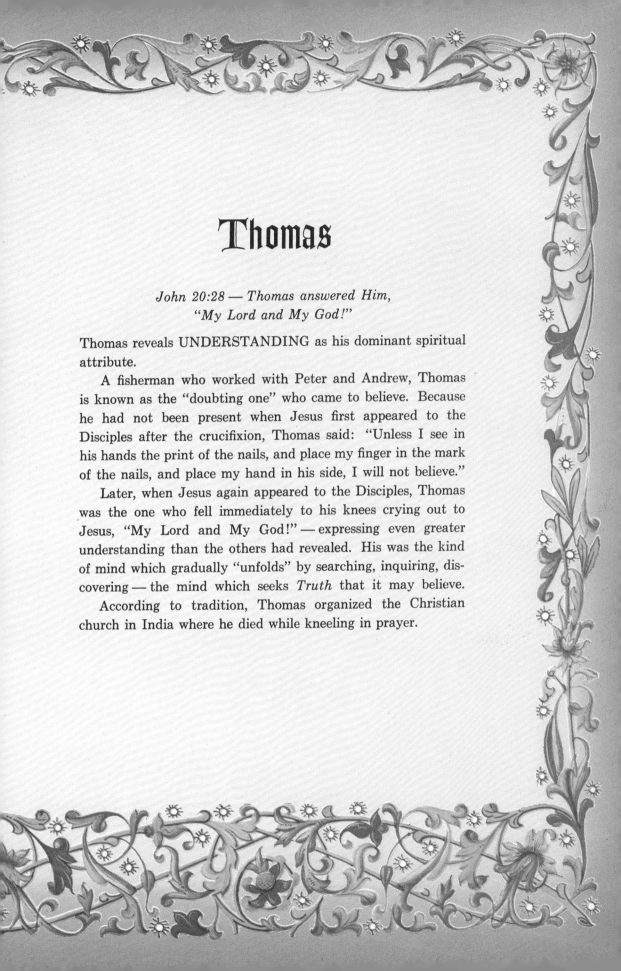

Thomas

John 20:28 — Thomas answered Him,
"My Lord and My God!"

Thomas reveals UNDERSTANDING as his dominant spiritual attribute.

A fisherman who worked with Peter and Andrew, Thomas is known as the "doubting one" who came to believe. Because he had not been present when Jesus first appeared to the Disciples after the crucifixion, Thomas said: "Unless I see in his hands the print of the nails, and place my finger in the mark of the nails, and place my hand in his side, I will not believe."

Later, when Jesus again appeared to the Disciples, Thomas was the one who fell immediately to his knees crying out to Jesus, "My Lord and My God!" — expressing even greater understanding than the others had revealed. His was the kind of mind which gradually "unfolds" by searching, inquiring, discovering — the mind which seeks *Truth* that it may believe.

According to tradition, Thomas organized the Christian church in India where he died while kneeling in prayer.

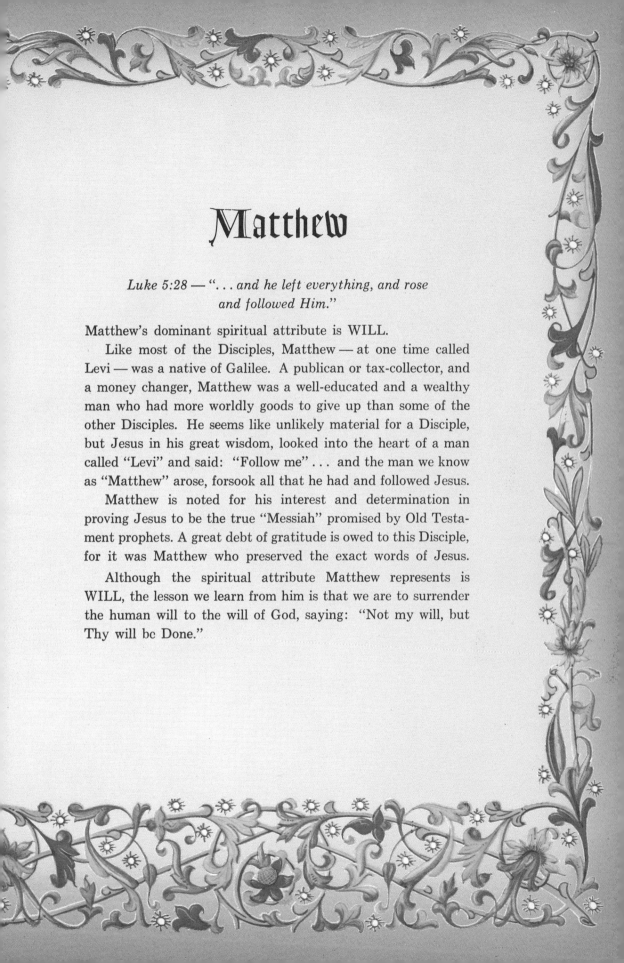

Matthew

Luke 5:28 — "... and he left everything, and rose and followed Him."

Matthew's dominant spiritual attribute is WILL.

Like most of the Disciples, Matthew — at one time called Levi — was a native of Galilee. A publican or tax-collector, and a money changer, Matthew was a well-educated and a wealthy man who had more worldly goods to give up than some of the other Disciples. He seems like unlikely material for a Disciple, but Jesus in his great wisdom, looked into the heart of a man called "Levi" and said: "Follow me" ... and the man we know as "Matthew" arose, forsook all that he had and followed Jesus.

Matthew is noted for his interest and determination in proving Jesus to be the true "Messiah" promised by Old Testament prophets. A great debt of gratitude is owed to this Disciple, for it was Matthew who preserved the exact words of Jesus.

Although the spiritual attribute Matthew represents is WILL, the lesson we learn from him is that we are to surrender the human will to the will of God, saying: "Not my will, but Thy will be Done."

James

(James the Less)

*Mark 3:18 — "... and Andrew and Philip, and Bar-
tholomew, and Matthew, and Thomas and James
the son of Alphaeus ..."*

James the Less has ORDER as his dominant spiritual attribute.

James was called "James the Less" because he was younger
than James, the brother of John. Since he is spoken of as
"James, the son of Alphaeus" in the Bible, scholars believe that
this man, whose true identity is still questioned, may have been
a cousin of Jesus.

James, who is said to have been the first bishop of Jerusalem,
was highly respected for his knowledge of law, and he represents
"law and order" in this series. Paul speaks of James the Less
as being in Jerusalem as the first Bishop, and he wrote that he
had visited James.

In the spiritual connotation, the attribute ORDER, as represented in the Disciple James the Less, means universal law and
order, or Principle.

James

(the Brother of John)

Mark I:19 — And going on a little farther, he saw James the son of Zebedee, and John his brother, who also were in the boat mending the nets.

James has WISDOM as the dominant spiritual attribute.

James was a fisherman, and fished with his father, Zebedee, and his brother John. The two brothers were called, "sons of thunder."

Representing wisdom and discernment, or good judgment, the vital spiritual faculties required for a balanced life, James was one of the three Disciples who were part of the "inner circle." He went with Jesus — as did John (love), and Peter (faith) — to the Garden of Gethsemane on the night before the crucifixion.

James did his missionary work in Spain, and has been the Patron Saint of Christian Spanish people. He was the first Disciple to suffer martyrdom; and upon his death, his body was returned to Spain.

The man who betrayed James was so impressed with the great faith of James, he became a Christian, and later, he too was condemned to death for his Christian beliefs.

Philip

John 1:44, 45 — Philip found Nathanael, and said to him, "We have found him, of whom Moses in the law, and also the prophets wrote, Jesus of Nazareth, the son of Joseph."

Philip's dominant spiritual attribute is POWER.

Because he knew the Greek language so well, Philip was called "the Greek," but he was "of Bethsaida, the city of Andrew and Peter," and he lived in Galilee as they did.

Philip, a powerful and vital man, was among the first to join the little band of men as a chosen Disciple of Jesus. He, it was, who brought Nathanael, or Bartholomew, to Jesus.

Philip, using the power of the Word, as he and the other Disciples were empowered to do in His name, healed the sick and cast out "unclean spirits." His difficulty in understanding the spiritual meaning of Jesus' message at times, did not seem to hinder his wonderful power to cure the lame and the paralyzed in this way.

According to traditional legend, Philip and Bartholomew traveled together after Pentecost, and Philip is said to have gone on as far as Phrygia.

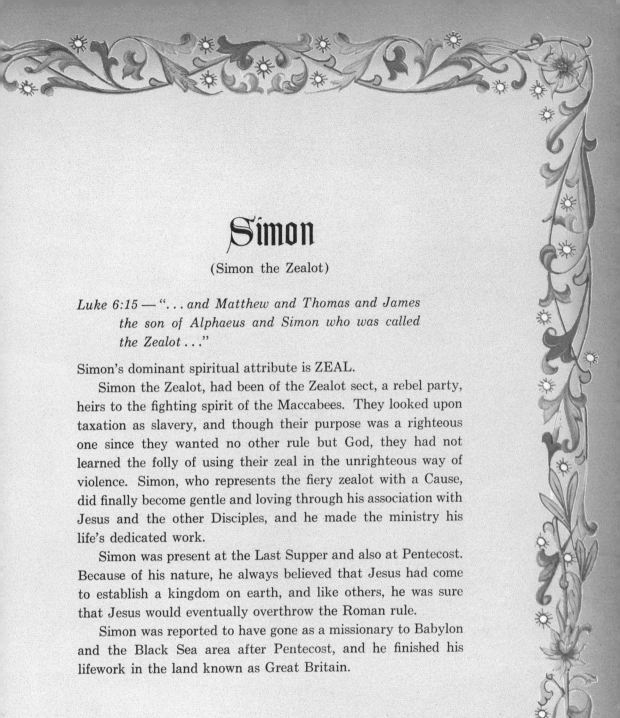

Simon

(Simon the Zealot)

Luke 6:15 — "... and Matthew and Thomas and James the son of Alphaeus and Simon who was called the Zealot ..."

Simon's dominant spiritual attribute is ZEAL.

Simon the Zealot, had been of the Zealot sect, a rebel party, heirs to the fighting spirit of the Maccabees. They looked upon taxation as slavery, and though their purpose was a righteous one since they wanted no other rule but God, they had not learned the folly of using their zeal in the unrighteous way of violence. Simon, who represents the fiery zealot with a Cause, did finally become gentle and loving through his association with Jesus and the other Disciples, and he made the ministry his life's dedicated work.

Simon was present at the Last Supper and also at Pentecost. Because of his nature, he always believed that Jesus had come to establish a kingdom on earth, and like others, he was sure that Jesus would eventually overthrow the Roman rule.

Simon was reported to have gone as a missionary to Babylon and the Black Sea area after Pentecost, and he finished his lifework in the land known as Great Britain.

Judas

(Judas Iscariot)

Matthew 27:4 — Judas, who betrayed Him . . . repented himself, and brought back the thirty pieces of silver . . . saying: "I have sinned in betraying innocent blood" . . . and he went away and hanged himself.

Judas represents the attribute LIFE, "redeemed" or betrayed."

Judas, who betrayed the Master, actually symbolizes the "Life Conserver," for the Judas function generates the life of the body. Judas governs the life consciousness, in the symbolic sense, and its lowest expression as "sensation" must be divinely guided and "redeemed," if the Christ is not to be betrayed.

Judas, who hoped that Jesus brought a "human" kingdom that would overthrow Roman rule, revealed high qualities or Jesus would not have chosen him for a Disciple. He trusted Judas enough to give him the money to provide places for the Disciples to sleep and eat on their travels. He trusted Judas to live up to his spiritual self.

At last, Judas betrayed Jesus for 30 pieces of silver — confident that Jesus would save himself at the last moment, for he had seen Jesus perform many miracles. When he realized that Jesus was not going to save himself, he repented and tried to return the silver to secure Jesus' release. When the chief priests and elders rejected him, Judas was filled with such great remorse he hanged himself.

Saint Paul

Paul of Tarsus was converted from an ardent adherent of Judaism into a flaming apostle of Jesus. He was not in the original twelve, and it is doubtful that he ever saw Jesus in the flesh, but how wonderfully grand was his experience of Him as Lord and Saviour.

Saint Paul, after his marvelous experience of Christ, wrote down this experience under the inspiration of the Holy Spirit. Definitely and beautifully he associated the Christ of his vision with the Jesus whom the other Apostles had known in Galilee.

In thought, in deed, in the utmost giving of himself as an advocate and witness, Paul was the man under God who translated the religion of Christianity into a world religion. He became the bridge that connected Jesus the Galilean and the Christ of universal appeal — and it was his personal knowledge of God in Christ which enabled him to build that enduring bridge.

Dominated, not so much by an idea, as by a Person, Saint Paul has proclaimed to all who read his words that one can have intimate spiritual intercourse with Christ the Lord. The evidence that he was speaking from first-hand knowledge was stamped upon his writings. "I know HIM whom I have believed," were his words to Timothy.

How richly he believed in the ultimate victory and triumphant reign of his Lord.

So may we believe!